Triceratops

and other Cretaceous Plant-Eaters

by Daniel Cohen

Capstone Press

MINNEAPOLIS

Printed in the United States of America.

Capstone Press • 2440 Fernbrook Lane • Minneapolis, MN 55447

Editorial Director	John Coughlan
Managing Editor	Tom Streissguth
Production Editor	James Stapleton
Book Design	Timothy Halldin

Library of Congress Cataloging-in-Publication Data

Cohen , Daniel, 1936-
  Triceratops and other Cretaceous plant-eaters/Daniel Cohen
    p. cm. -- (Dinosaurs of North America)
    Includes bibliographical references (p. 41) and index.
    Summary: Describes what is known about three different types of dinosaurs that lived in parts of the United States and Canada from 140 to 65 million years ago.
    ISBN 1-56065-289-6
    1. Triceratops--Juvenile literature. 2. Parasaurolophus--Juvenile literature. 3. Maiasaura--Juvenile literature.
[1. Triceratops. 2. Parasaurolophus. 3. Maiasaura.
4. Dinosaurs.] I. Title. II. Series: Cohen, Daniel, 1936-
Dinosaurs of North America.
QE862.O65C63 1996
567.9'7--dc20   95-11244
                                                      CIP
                                                       AC

Table of Contents

Chapter 1
When They Lived

Millions and millions of years ago, huge herds of horned and duck-billed dinosaurs roamed what is now the North American continent. These **herbivorous** (plant-eating) dinosaurs were pursued by the largest, fiercest **carnivorous** (meat-eating) dinosaurs the world had ever known.

Then, quite suddenly, all of the dinosaurs were gone. Why? Was the earth struck by **asteroids** or a giant **comet**? Did a nearby star explode? No one knows.

Most of the **species** that have ever existed on earth are now gone. Species become extinct

Quaternary Age
1.8m to present

65m Tertiary Age 1.8m

140m Cretaceous Age 65m

195m Jurassic Age 140m

230m Triassic Age 195m

280m Permian Age 230m

345m Carboniferous 280m

395m Devonian Age 345m

435m Silurian Age 395m

500m Ordovcian Age 435m

700m Cambrian Age 500m

Birds

Mammals

Reptiles

Amphibians

Fish

Primitive chordat

and new ones evolve to take their place. But the sudden extinction of so many different species that had been so successful for so long seems unnatural.

The speculation on what happened continues. And it will continue for a long time. All we know for certain is that 65 million years ago, the dinosaurs that had dominated the earth disappeared.

Paleontologists–scientists who study ancient life on earth–divide the history of life into three great eras. They are the **Paleozoic** (pail-ee-oh-ZO-ic), or ancient life, era; the **Mesozoic** (mez-oh-ZO-ic), or middle life, era; and the **Cenozoic** (sen-oh-ZO-ic), or recent life, era.

The dinosaurs lived during the Mesozoic era, which is often called the Age of Dinosaurs. The Mesozoic era itself is divided into three periods. First is the **Triassic** (try-ASS-ic) period, from 230 million to 195 million years ago. Dinosaurs first began to appear late in the Triassic period.

The next period was the **Jurassic** (joo-RASS-ic) period, from 195 million to 140 million years ago. Dinosaurs flourished during this period, and the largest dinosaurs in history lived during this time.

The third period was the **Cretaceous** (cret-AY-shus) period, from 140 million to 65 million years ago. New types of dinosaurs appeared and the creatures were more numerous and successful than ever before.

A paleontologist studies skeletons, fossils, and other remains of prehistoric life.

The Cretaceous period was a time of great change on the earth. At one time, all of the earth's land mass was clumped together in a single supercontinent. This land mass began to split apart during the Jurassic period. This split accelerated during the Cretaceous period.

The Cretaceous period was also a time of enormous volcanic upheaval. Mountain ranges appeared and new islands were formed. The earth's climate changed dramatically as well. The seasons became more pronounced. There were more storms. The moist and tropical conditions of the Jurassic period no longer prevailed over the entire earth.

The drifting of the continents, the formation of mountain ranges, and the harsher climate meant that dinosaurs could no longer freely roam the world. The range of many of the later Cretaceous dinosaurs was more limited than it had been during the Jurassic period.

As the earth changed, so did the animals and plants. Early in dinosaur history, the creatures ate mainly ferns, palms, and cycads, which are

9

primitive plants. By the late Cretaceous period, flowering plants and trees had evolved. Oaks, hickories, and other tree families began to appear in cooler areas where the more primitive plants could not survive.

New species of turtles, snakes, and other reptiles developed. Amphibians like frogs and salamanders first appeared during the Cretaceous period. Herons, gulls, and plovers, birds that evolved during the Cretaceous, are still familiar today.

A Maiasaura, whose name means good mother lizard, tends its nest of young.

Mammals and dinosaurs had evolved at about the same time during the Triassic period. The mammals continued to thrive during the Cretaceous period, but they remained small. They had changed very little from the mammals of earlier times. They would not really develop or dominate until the dinosaurs became extinct.

That brings us back to the question of the extinction of the dinosaurs at the end of the Cretaceous period. While the earth had certainly changed during this period, the dinosaurs appeared able to adapt well to the changes. New species of dinosaurs evolved to take advantage of the changing conditions.

Then, at the end of the Cretaceous period, all the dinosaurs suddenly died out. This appears to have happened very quickly. Though many theories about the extinction of the dinosaurs have been offered by scientists, there is no universal agreement on what happened. The extinction of the dinosaurs remains one of the most puzzling mysteries of science.

Triceratops

(try-SER-ah-tops)
three-horned face
Range: *Western United States and Canada*
Length: *30 feet (9 meters)*
Weight: *6 tons (5.4 metric tons)*

The most common large plant-eating dinosaurs of the late Cretaceous period in western North America were the **ceratopsids** (ser-a-TOP-sids). They were found nowhere else in the world.

The word, which means horn faced, fits these massive four-legged dinosaurs. They had huge heads, and a bony frill, developed from the rear skull bones, protected their neck. Different species had from one to a dozen

A Triceratops had only its bony horns to defend itself against the powerful Tyrannosaurus rex.

sharp horns growing from their snout, head, or from the bony frill.

The pillarlike legs and heavy, hoofed feet supported a stocky body that was covered with a tough, thick hide. Scientists now believe that

these dinosaurs could run at speeds of up to 30 miles (48 kilometers) per hour, at least for a short distance. The modern animal they resemble most is the rhinoceros. But the dinosaurs were much bigger.

A charging dinosaur of this type would have been a terrifying foe. In that time, dinosaurs needed all the protection they could get. The Cretaceous world was a dangerous one.

All the evidence suggests that these dinosaurs found safety in numbers. They moved in great herds through the forests. When threatened by some of the great predators of the period, like Tyrannosaurus, they could have formed a circle with their horned heads facing outward toward the danger. The smaller and weaker young would be in the center. That would have been an effective defense, even against the fearsome Tyrannosaurus.

These dinosaurs did not have teeth. They foraged through the upland forests chopping off vegetation with their sharp, toothless, beaklike mouths. They adapted to take advantage of the newly evolved and tougher vegetation of the late Cretaceous.

Of all the horned dinosaurs, the best known, and probably the most numerous, was Triceratops. It was also the largest dinosaur of

Triceratops had a huge head and a bony frill that protected the neck.

this type. A full-grown Triceratops weighed more than a modern African bull elephant, today's largest land animal. Its skull alone, with its short neck frill, was more than six feet (1.8 meters) long. It had a short, thick nose horn and two long horns higher on its head.

These horns could have measured more than three feet (90 centimeters) each.

Scientists were confused when the first fragmentary remains of this creature were discovered. When the great fossil collector Othniel Charles Marsh was shown the horns of a Triceratops, he thought they belonged to an

extinct species of buffalo. Marsh was wrong. A few years later one of his associates found a full skull of one of the creatures. Marsh realized the horns came from a long-extinct dinosaur, not a dead buffalo.

Because of the massive structure of Triceratops's skull, it was more likely to be preserved than the bones of other, weaker dinosaurs. Hundreds of well-preserved Triceratops specimens have been found over the years in the western United States and Canada. The American fossil hunter Barnum Brown is said to have collected more than 500 skulls of this particular dinosaur. Today more than 15 species of Triceratops are recognized. Fossilized remains of this dinosaur can be found in most large and many small museum collections.

Many of the skulls, horns, and neck frills were found to be damaged and scarred. This suggests that individual Triceratops often sparred with one another. Perhaps they locked horns and shoved one another with their head shields, rather than doing actual damage with their sharp horns. These dangerous weapons were probably only used on real enemies like Tyrannosaurus.

Fossils show that Triceratops continued to flourish right up to the end of the Cretaceous period. It may well have been the last surviving large dinosaur in the western part of North America, and perhaps the last surviving large dinosaur in the entire world. But it, too, mysteriously died off at the end of the Cretaceous period, along with all other dinosaurs.

Hadrosaurs like Parasaurolophus spent most of their time walking on all fours looking for food.

Parasaurolophus

(pair-ah-SAW-roh-LOH-fus)
similar crested lizard
Range: *Western United States and Canada*
Length: *30 feet (9 meters)*
Weight: *4 tons (3.6 metric tons)*

The **hadrosaurs** (HAD-row-sawrs), commonly called duck-billed dinosaurs, were one of the last large groups of dinosaurs to develop. They appeared in the middle of the Cretaceous period and evolved into a wide variety of types. They were a successful group and eventually spread throughout the northern hemisphere.

A museum exhibit shows models of a Maiasaura family.

These dinosaurs had long faces with broad, flattened, toothless snouts. That is why they are called duck-billed. Toward the back of their mouths were rows of strong teeth, hundreds of them in each jaw. New teeth continually replaced old, worn ones. This was a unique development among dinosaurs and probably accounted for the group's success. They were well adapted to eating the new and tougher plants that appeared during the Cretaceous period.

All hadrosaurs had long hind legs and shorter forelegs with hooflike nails for walking. These dinosaurs probably spent most of their time walking on all fours looking for food. When it came time to run from predators, they would have reared up on their hind legs and sprinted away. They would have used their long tails for balance.

Many hadrosaurs had bony crests on the top of their heads. These crests came in a variety of shapes and sizes. Of all the hadrosaurs, Parasaurolophus had the most striking head

ornament. It was a backward pointing, hornlike crest mounted on the back of the skull. In some individuals the crest extended more than three feet (90 centimeters) beyond the back of the skull.

Though the crest of Parasaurolophus looks rather like a horn, it is hollow. It would have been much too fragile to be used in a fight. Besides, it is in the wrong place. The crest is so far back on the skull that it is hard to imagine how it could have been used in fighting.

What were the crests used for? Many different theories have been proposed over the years.

At one time it was believed that the hadrosaurs spent much of their time in the

Hadrosaurs such as Parasaurolophus spread through the northern hemisphere, from Mexico to Canada.

27

water. According to this theory, the hollow crest could have served as an underwater

A museum model shows a partial Parasaurolophus skeleton, with a wall drawing to show what the entire skeleton must have looked like.

breathing device. But scientists now believe that was not the case.

Another suggestion has been that the hollow crests provided an enlarged area for sensory

glands. As defenseless plant-eaters, hadrosaurs would have needed sharp senses. Hearing, sight, and smell would have given them warnings of the approach of predators.

But there are problems with this theory as well. If the crests held sensory glands that helped the hadrosaurs escape predators, why did the hadrosaurs with small crests, or no crests at all, survive just as well as Parasaurolophus and others with enormous crests?

The most popular theory today is that the crests were probably used as signaling devices to allow different hadrosaurs to recognize members of their own species. Most hadrosaurs are about the same size and shape. Many different hadrosaur species lived in the same area. The crests are so strikingly different that it would not have been hard to tell one from the other, even at a distance. The crests may also have been brightly colored.

Hadrosaurs apparently had excellent hearing. Parasaurolophus's hollow crest was

connected to its nose. If it breathed out strongly, the hollow crest would have helped to create a loud honking sound. Different species with different crests would have produced very different sounds. These individualized sounds would have allowed herds to keep in contact even when they could not see one another.

The late Cretaceous period might have been a very colorful and noisy time in earth's history.

Maiasaura

(my-a-SAW-ra)
good mother lizard
Range*: Western United States and Canada*
Length*: 30 feet (9 meters)*
Weight*: 4 tons (3.6 metric tons)*

For more than a century after dinosaurs were first discovered, scientists regarded them as little more than giant reptiles. The dinosaurs were thought to be slow moving and rather stupid. It was believed that they laid their eggs and then walked away, like most reptiles. After

A mother Maiasaura tends her nest of babies. Like some modern reptiles, the Maiasaura was protective of its young.

hatching in the heat of the sun, the young immediately had to fend for themselves.

Many of the old beliefs about dinosaurs have changed as the result of new discoveries. In 1978 a remarkable discovery in western Montana changed our view of how dinosaurs cared for their young. John Horner and Robert Makela reported finding the nesting site of a new species of hadrosaur. This new dinosaur was given the name Maiasaura, or good mother lizard.

Horner and Makela had found the remains of a complete nesting site. It was a 75 million-year-old dinosaur nursery, where this species of duck-billed dinosaur laid its eggs and where the young were able to develop and grow in safety.

Before this find, little was known about dinosaur reproduction. In the 1920s, the first dinosaur eggs were discovered in Mongolia. They belonged to Protoceratops, a small relation of the horned dinosaurs. The nests had been carefully dug in the sand. The eggs inside

them were very well preserved, considering they were 70 million years old. But this find, sensational as it was, did not tell us nearly as much about dinosaur behavior as the 1978 discovery.

What the scientists found in Montana was the skeleton of an adult dinosaur, perhaps the mother, several youngsters about three feet (90 centimeters) long, and some newly hatched

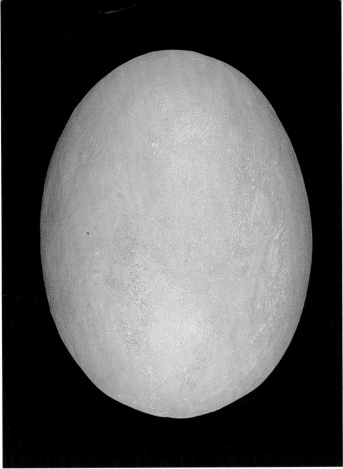

Scientists have discovered that Maiasauras carefully built nests for their eggs and their young.

dinosaurs. The hatchlings were in a nest. Nearby were several other nests with eggs and pieces of broken shell scattered around.

The nests had clearly been prepared with great care. Inside the nest, the eggs had been

laid in circles, layer upon layer. The mother probably covered each layer with sand or dirt, and then covered the whole nest the same way. This would have kept the eggs warm. It would also help conceal the eggs from marauding egg stealers.

The females nested in groups, showing that they were social animals. Evidence also shows that the dinosaurs returned to the same nesting site year after year. The young dinosaurs also stayed with their mother until they were mature enough to take care of themselves. The youngsters stayed near the nest while the mother, and perhaps the father, brought food to them.

None of this evidence should have been very surprising. Such modern reptiles as crocodiles guard their nests and their young. Birds, which may be closely related to dinosaurs, certainly do. Many birds and reptiles have communal nesting sites to which they return year after year.

The discovery of a Maiasaura nesting colony changed modern attitudes toward dinosaurs.

But in 1978 this information about Maiasaura nesting habits was surprising. At that time most people believed that dinosaurs were just too stupid to do anything as complicated as raising young. The discovery went a long way toward changing modern attitudes toward dinosaurs.

Since 1978 nesting colonies of other types of dinosaurs have been discovered. But nothing has matched the dramatic evidence found in the Maiasaura colony in Montana.

Glossary

asteroid–one of thousands of small planets or fragments of planets in our solar system

carnivorous–having the ability to eat and digest meat

Cenozoic–the era of recent life from 65 million years ago to the present

ceratopsid–a horn-faced dinosaur

comet–a body made up of frozen gas and rock that passes through our solar system

Cretaceous period–the third geological period in the Age of Dinosaurs, from 140 million to 65 million years ago

hadrosaur–a duck-billed dinosaur

herbivorous–describes a species that lives on plants and vegetation

Jurassic period–the second geological period in the Age of Dinosaurs, from 195 million to 140 million years ago

Mesozoic–the era of middle life, or the Age of Dinosaurs, from 230 million to 65 million years ago

paleontologists–scientists who study life in past ages

Paleozoic–the era of ancient life from 600 million to 230 million years ago

species–a group of animals that look the same and can breed together

Triassic period–the first geological period in the Age of Dinosaurs, from 230 million to 195 million years ago

To Learn More

Arnold, Caroline. *Dinosaur Mountain: Graveyard of the Past.* New York: Clarion Books, 1989.

Benton, Michael. *The Dinosaur Encyclopedia.* New York: Julian Messner, 1984.

Berenstain, Michael. *The Horned Dinosaur, Triceratops.* Racine, WI: Western Publishing Co., 1989.

Cohen, Daniel and Cohen, Susan. *Where to Find Dinosaurs Today.* New York: Cobblehill, 1992.

Lasky, Kathryn. *Dinosaur Dig.* New York: Morrow Junior Books, 1990.

Lauber, Patricia. *Dinosaurs Walked Here and other Stories Fossils Tell.* New York: Bradbury Press, 1991.

Lindsay, William. *The Great Dinosaur Atlas.* New York: Julian Messner, 1991.

Murphy, Jim. *The Last Dinosaur.* New York: Scholastic, 1988.

Riehecky, Janet. *Maiasaura.* Chicago: Childrens Press, 1989.

Sandell, Elizabeth J. *Maiasaura: The Good Mother Dinosaur.* Mankato, Minn: Bancroft-Sage Publications, 1988.

Steffof, Rebecca. *Extinction.* New York: Chelsea House Publishers, 1992.

Wallace, Joseph E. *The Audubon Society Pocket Guide to Dinosaurs.* New York: Knopf, 1992.

Some Useful Addresses

The Academy of Natural Sciences
19th Street and The Parkway
Philadelphia, PA 19103

The American Museum of Natural History
Central Park West at 79th Street
New York, NY 10024-5192

California Academy of Sciences
Golden Gate Park
San Francisco, CA 94118-4599

Dinosaur National Monument
P.O. Box 210
Dinosaur, CO 81610

Field Museum of Natural History
Roosevelt Road at Lake Shore Drive
Chicago, IL 60605-2496

Museum of the Rockies
South Sixth Street and Kagy Boulevard
Bozeman, MT 59717-0040

National Museum of Natural History
Smithsonian Institution
Tenth Street and Constitution Avenue N.W.
Washington, DC 20002

**Natural History Museum of Los Angeles
  County**
900 Exposition Blvd.
Los Angeles, CA 90007

New Mexico Museum of Natural History
1801 Mountain Road
Albuquerque, NM 87104

The Peabody Museum
170 Whitney Avenue
New Haven, CT 06511

Royal Ontario Museum
100 Queen's Park
Toronto, Ontario M5S 2C6
Canada

Tyrell Museum of Paleontology
Box 7500
Drumheller, Alberta T0J 0Y0
Canada

Where to View Dinosaur Tracks

Dinosaur Ridge

This is a national landmark near Morrison, west of Denver, Colorado. The hiking trail allows visitors to stroll along a trackbed from the Cretaceous period.

Dinosaur Valley State Park

This park is in Glen Rose, southwest of Fort Worth, Texas. Part of an original dinosaur trackway was excavated here. It is on view at the American Museum of Natural History in New York City.

Dinosaur State Park

Visitors to this park, in Rocky Hill, south of Hartford, Connecticut, can make plaster casts of dinosaur tracks.

For more information on dinosaur events and sites, write to:

Dinosaur Society
200 Carleton Avenue
East Islip, NY 11730
(516) 277-7855

This organization promotes research and education in the study of dinosaurs. It also publishes *Dino Times*, a monthly magazine for children. Subscriptions are $19.95 a year. *Dinosaur Report*, a quarterly magazine, costs $25 a year.

Photo credits: Linda J. Moore: p. 4; Bruce Selyem, Museum of the Rockies: pp. 8, 12, 24, 32, 35; James P. Rowan: p. 10-11; Denver Museum of Natural History: p. 20; John Weinstein, The Field Museum, Chicago IL: p. 28-29 (Neg #GEO-85859.4c); The Field Museum, Chicago, IL: p. 14 (Neg. #GEO 85828), (Neg, #59442) pp. 16-17; Museum of the Rockies: p. 36.

Index